Let's Classify and Fold Origami Animals

Let's Classify and Fold ORIGAMI FISH

by Ruth Owen

Enslow PUBLISHING

Published in 2023 by Enslow Publishing, LLC
29 East 21st Street, New York, NY 10010

Produced for Rosen by Ruth Owen Books
Designer: Emma Randall
Photos courtesy of Ruth Owen Books and Shutterstock

Cataloging-in-Publication Data

Names: Owen, Ruth.
Title: Let's classify and fold origami fish / Ruth Owen.
Description: New York : Enslow Publishing, 2023. | Series: Let's classify and fold origami animals | Includes glossary and index.
Identifiers: ISBN 9781978530102 (pbk.) | ISBN 9781978530126 (library bound) | ISBN 9781978530119 (6pack) | ISBN 9781978530133 (ebook)
Subjects: LCSH: Fishes in art--Juvenile literature. | Origami--Juvenile literature.
Classification: LCC TT872.5 O937 2023 | DDC 736´.982--dc23

Manufactured in the United States of America

Please visit our website, www.enslowpublishing.com. For a free color catalog of all our high-quality books, call toll free 1-800-398-2504 or fax 1-877-980-4454

CPSIA compliance information: Batch #CSENS23: For further information contact Enslow Publishing LLC, New York, New York at 1-800-398-2504.

Find us on

Contents

Meet the Fish

Fish come in many different shapes and sizes. Some **species** are tiny—less than half an inch (1.25 cm) long. The whale shark is the largest fish and can grow to 40 feet (12 m) long. Scientists think there are more than 34,000 different species of fish.

A whale shark

Fish have five main characteristics.

All fish spend their lives in water. Some species live in salty oceans, seas, and lakes. Others are found in freshwater rivers, lakes, and ponds.

Fish are **vertebrates**, which means they have a backbone, or spine.

A fish skeleton

Almost all fish are **ectothermic**, or cold-blooded. This means a fish's body cannot **regulate** its inner temperature. As the water around a fish gets warmer or colder, a fish's inner body temperature goes up or down, too.

Fish breathe underwater through body parts called **gills**. They suck in water through their mouths and then pass it out through their gills. The gills absorb **oxygen** from the water.

Some types of fish have skin that's covered with scales.

Ready to discover more about fish? Then grab some origami paper and let's get folding and learning all about fish!

Living Together: Tropical Fish

Some species of fish live together in large groups called schoals and schools. A schoal is a group of fish, such as tropical fish, that swim and live close together. Each fish in the schoal does its own thing, searching for food or hiding from **predators**.

In a school, the fish travel in a **synchronized** way, swimming in the same direction, twisting and turning, and hunting as a team. A single school of herring may be made up of one billion fish. Living in such an enormous group could be a way for each fish to reduce its chances of being caught by a predator.

A school of herring

A schoal of tropical fish

FOLD A TROPICAL FISH

You will need:

- A square piece of paper in your choice of color or pattern
- A marker

Step 1:
Place the paper patterned side down. Fold the paper in half, and crease.

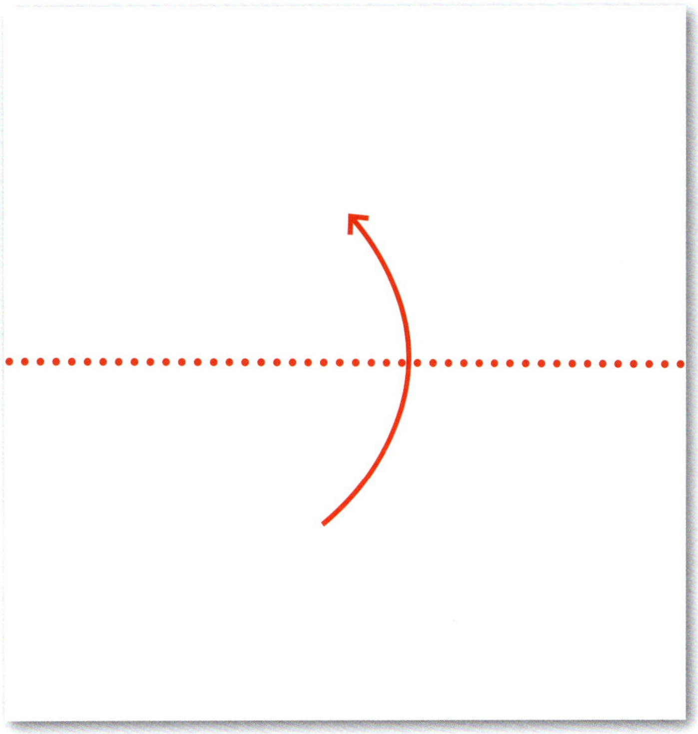

Step 2:

Fold the paper in half again to create a square.

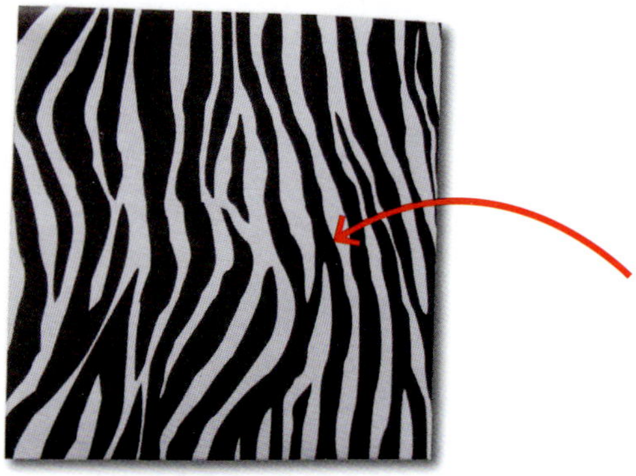

Step 3:

Now open out the square's top layer of paper to create a pocket. Gently squash and flatten the pocket to make a triangle.

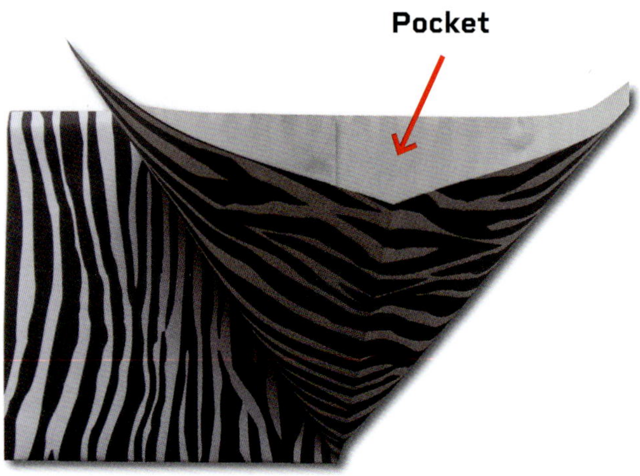

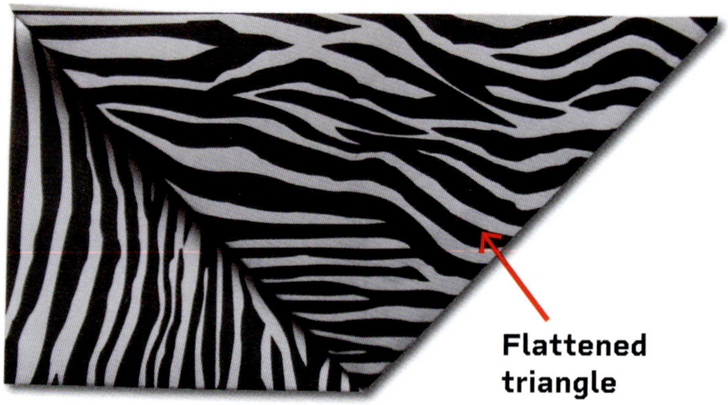

Step 4:

Turn the model over. Open out the right-hand side of the model to create a pocket.

Then gently squash and flatten the pocket to make a triangle.

Step 5:
Turn the triangle on its side. Fold down the top point of the triangle along the dotted line and crease. You should only fold the top layer of paper.

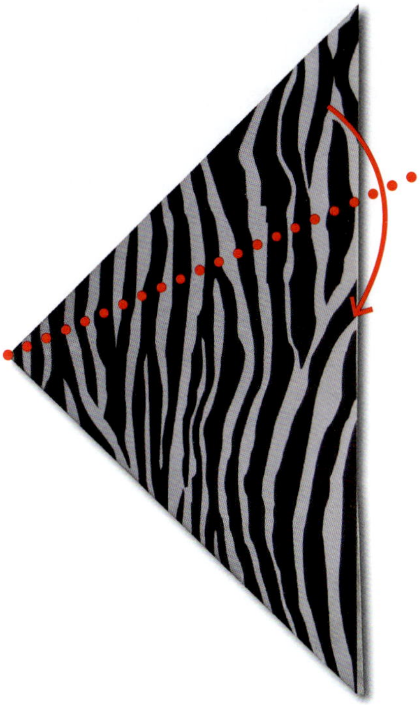

Step 6:
Fold up the bottom point of the model along the dotted line, and crease.

Step 7:
Flip your model over and your tropical fish is complete. If you wish, draw on an eye.

Built for Swimming: Fish Bodies

A fish swims using body parts called fins. It has a dorsal fin on its back. This fin helps keep the fish upright and keeps it from rolling over. The dorsal fin also helps the fish make turns. The caudal, or tail, fin propels the fish through water and helps it to steer.

A fish has a pair of pelvic fins on the bottom of its body. They help it balance and stay upright. A fish also has a pair of pectoral fins. These fins are positioned one on each side of its body close to its gills—a little like the wings of a plane. A fish uses its pectoral fins for steering.

FOLD A FISH WITH FINS

You will need:

- A square piece of paper in your choice of color or pattern

Step 1:
Fold the paper in half to form a rectangle.

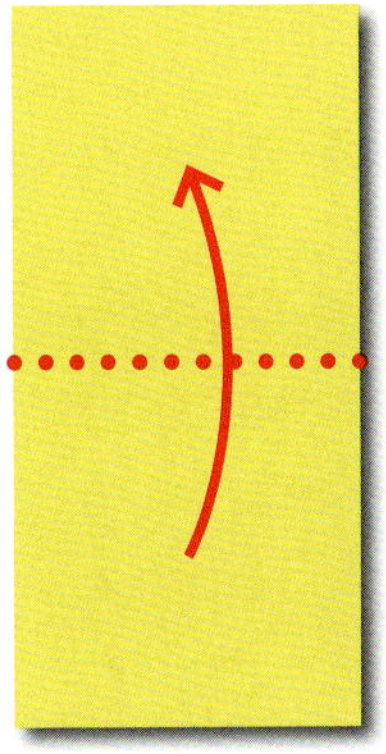

Fold the rectangle in half to form a small square.

Step 2:
Next, fold the small square in half, crease, and then unfold.

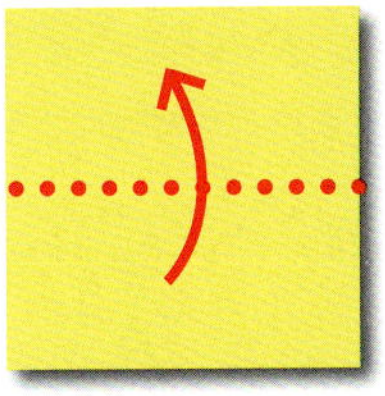

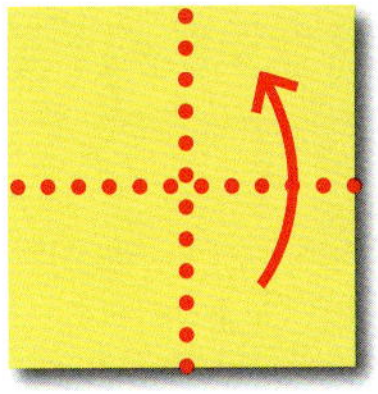

Turn the square 90 degrees clockwise. Then fold in half again, crease, and unfold.

Step 3:
Next, fold the square in half diagonally along one of the dotted lines, crease, and unfold. Then fold diagonally along the other dotted line, and crease.

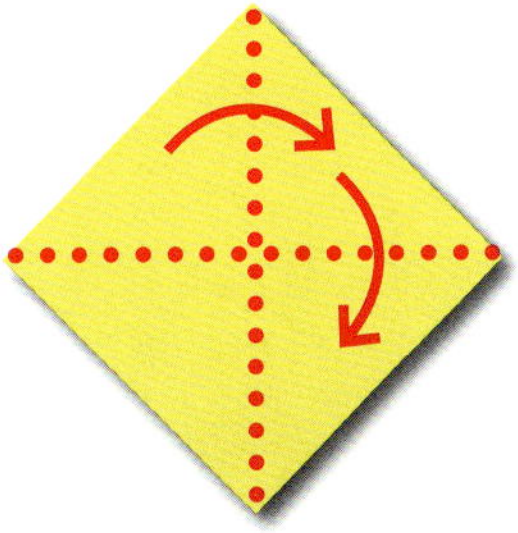

Now open the paper. It should look like this.

Step 4:

Fold down the top quarter of the paper. Then open out the top left-hand corner, and then squash it flat to form a triangle, or point.

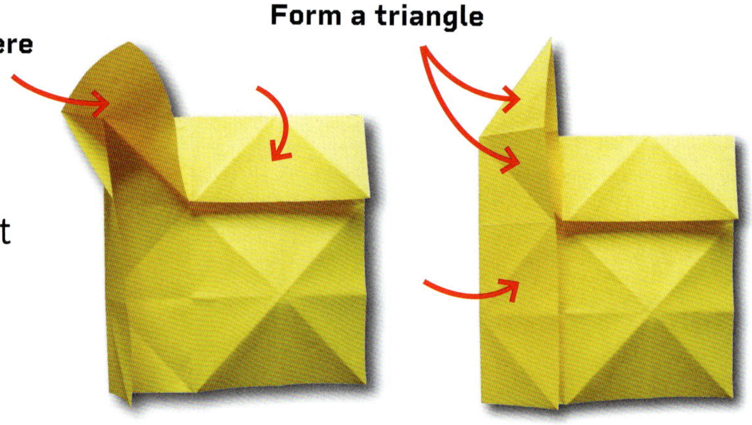

As you do this, the left-hand side of the paper will fold in, too.

Step 5:

Next, fold up the bottom quarter of the paper. Open out the left-hand corner, and then squash it flat to form a point.

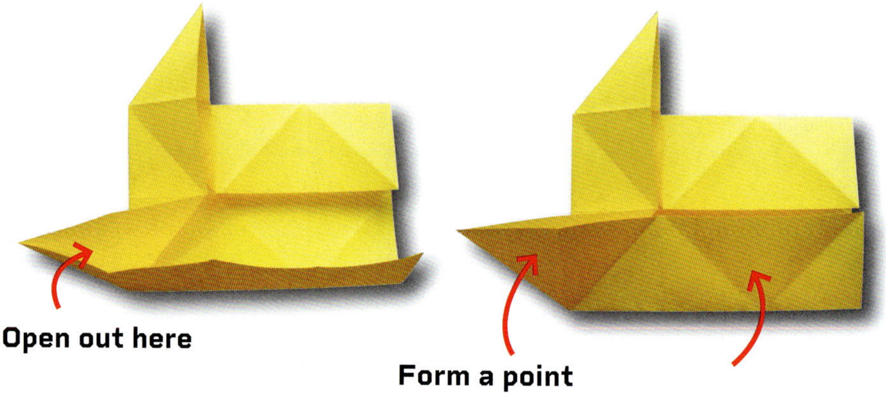

Step 6:

Now fold in the right-hand quarter of the model. Then open out the bottom corner, and squash it flat to form a point.

Step 7:

Finally, open out the top right-hand corner, and squash it flat to form a fourth point.

Step 8:
Now, fold up the bottom point.

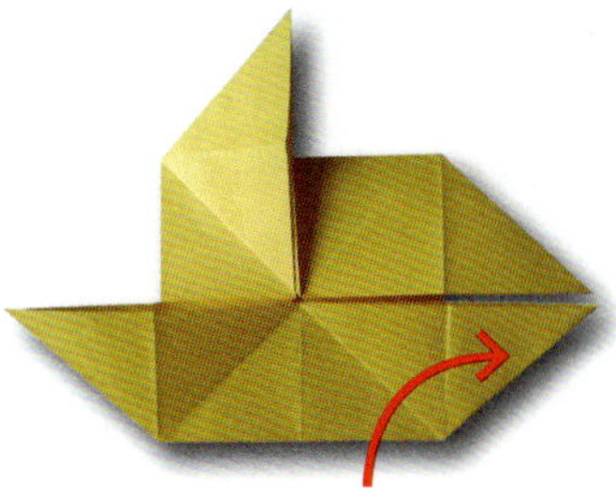

Step 9:
Next, fold down the left-hand point.

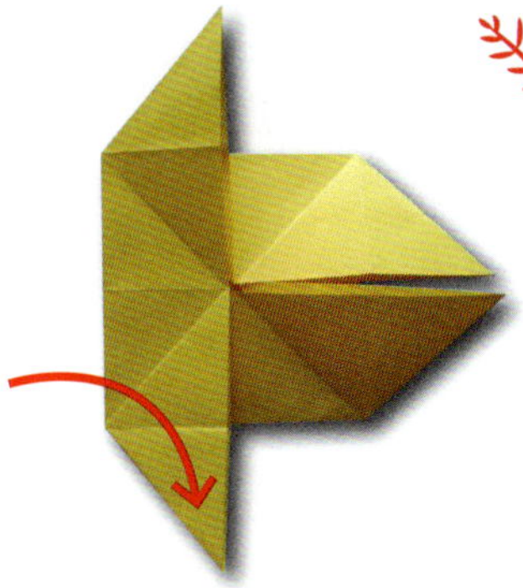

Step 10:
Now, fold up the bottom right-hand point along the dotted line, and crease hard.

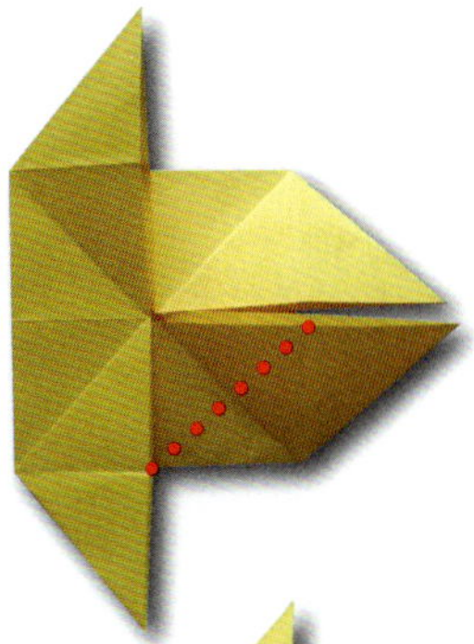

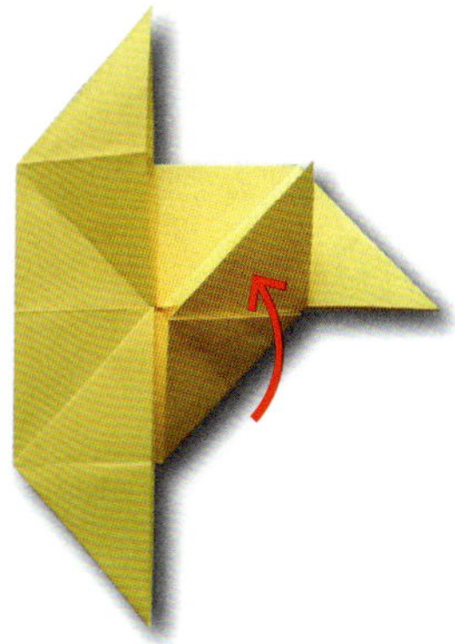

Then fold just the top part of the point back down.

Repeat what you've just done on the top right-hand point. Your model should now look like this.

Step 11:
Fold down the top left-hand point, as shown. Then fold up the bottom left-hand point.

space for mouth

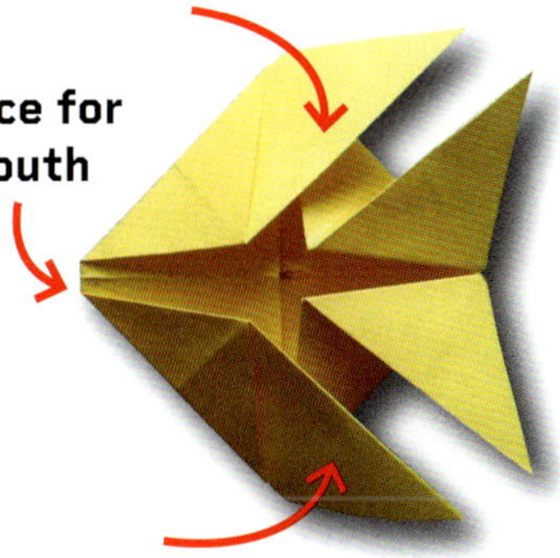

Leave a small space between these two folds to form a mouth.

Step 12:
Turn the model over and your fish with fins is complete!

Predators with Swords: Swordfish

A swordfish is a large, predatory fish that uses its long, swordlike bill to slash at herring and other fish. Once a swordfish has injured its **prey**, it starts feeding. Swordfish live mostly in warm waters in the Atlantic Ocean, Pacific Ocean, and Indian Ocean. They can grow to more than 10 feet (3 m) long.

Some members of the fish family give birth to live babies, but most lay eggs. A female swordfish lays millions of eggs at one time. Just two days later, tiny baby swordfish, or **larvae**, hatch from the eggs.

FOLD A SWORDFISH

You will need:

- One square piece of blue or gray paper
- A black marker

Step 1:
Fold the paper in half diagonally, and crease.

Step 2:
Fold the right-hand point of the model into the center, and crease.

Turn the model over, fold the new right-hand point of the model into the center, and crease.

Step 3:
Now slide your fingers into the center "pocket" of the model. Gently open out the pocket to form a beak-like shape, then squash the model flat to create a triangle.

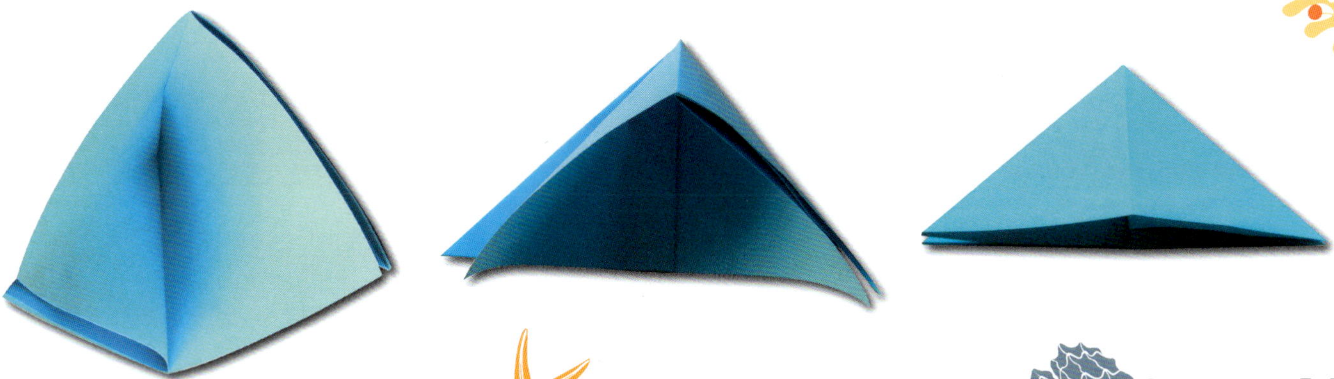

Step 4:

Now take hold of the top layer of paper on the right-hand side of the triangle and fold the point into the center. Crease well, and then unfold.

Step 5:

Take hold of the top layer of paper on the left-hand side and make a fold that follows the line of the crease you made in step 4. Crease well, and then unfold.

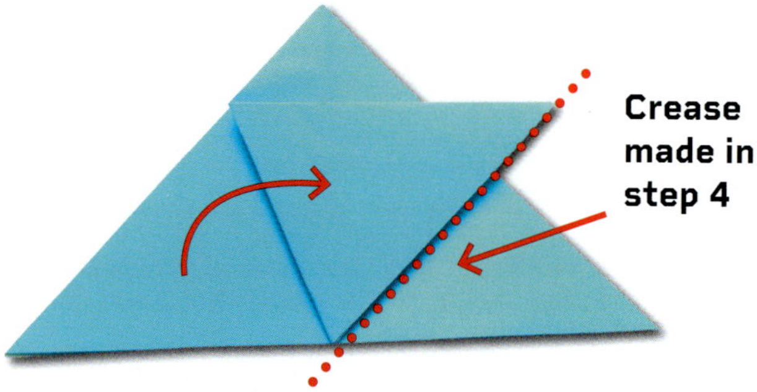

Step 6:

Take hold of the top layer of paper on the left-hand side and make a new fold, this time following the line of the crease you made in step 5.

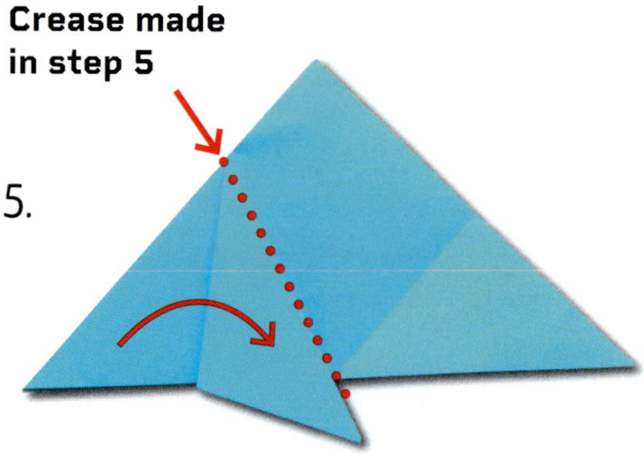

Step 7:

Now make a small fold along the dotted line and crease well.

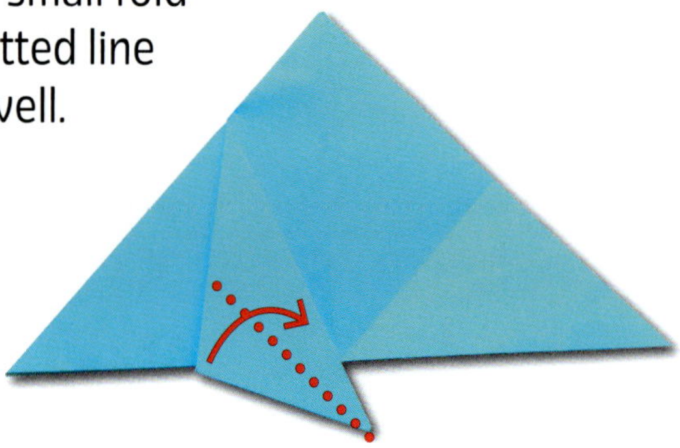

Step 8:

Now fold down the top half of the model along the dotted line.

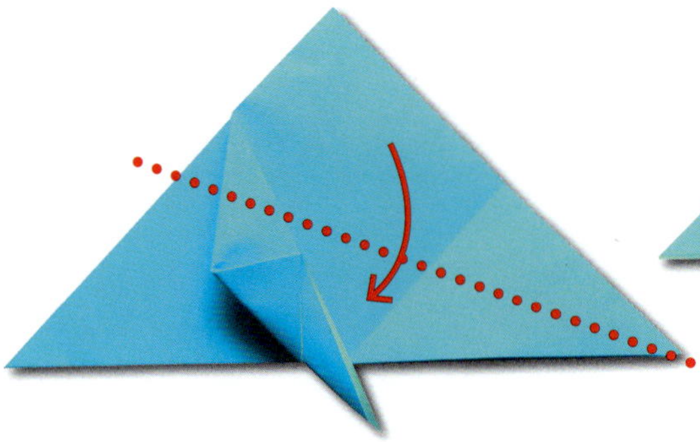

Your model should look like this.

Step 9:
Now fold the center point of the model upward along the dotted line.

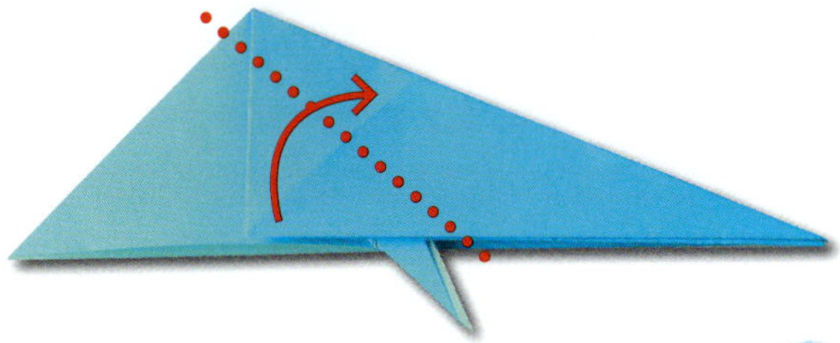

Step 10:
To make the fish's pointed sword, fold down the left-hand top edge of the model and fold up the left-hand bottom edge of the model.

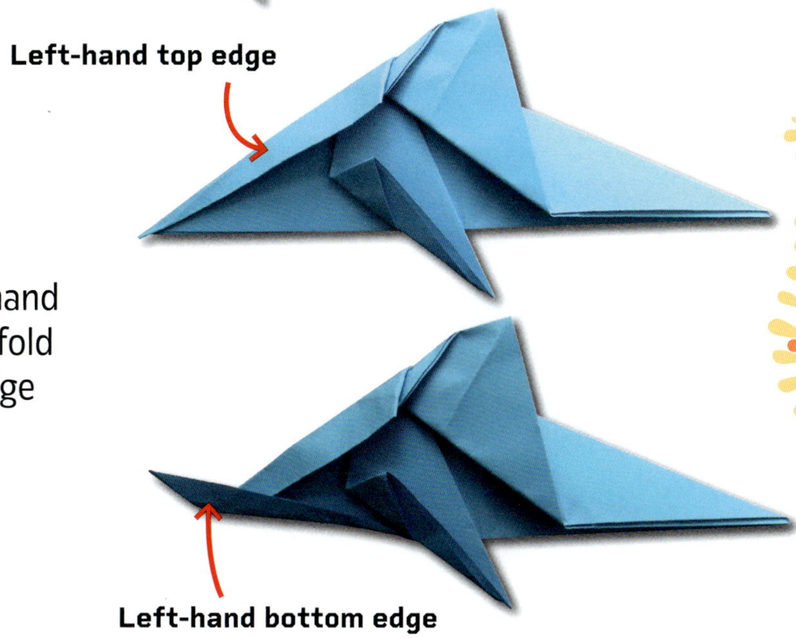

Step 11:
Turn the model over and twist the snout into the "sword" shape.

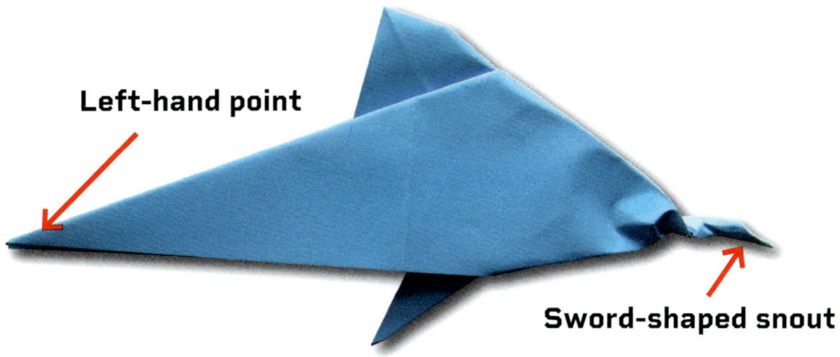

Step 12:
To make the tail, fold down and reverse fold the left-hand point.

Then open out and separate the two points of the tail.

Finish your model by drawing on a face.

A Defensive Sting: Stingrays

A stingray is a fish with a long, whiplike tail that is armed with a razor-sharp weapon known as a sting, or spine. The spear-like sting has serrated edges like the edges of a saw. It is made from **cartilage** and grows from the fish's tail like a long fingernail.

A stringray uses its sting to defend itself from predators, such as sharks. If a stingray is threatened by a predator, it flips its long tail toward its enemy, and sinks the sting into its victim's flesh. The sting then delivers a shot of **venom** into the attacker.

FOLD A STINGRAY

You will need:

- A square piece of paper in your choice of color
- Markers

Step 1:

Fold the paper in half diagonally, crease, and unfold.

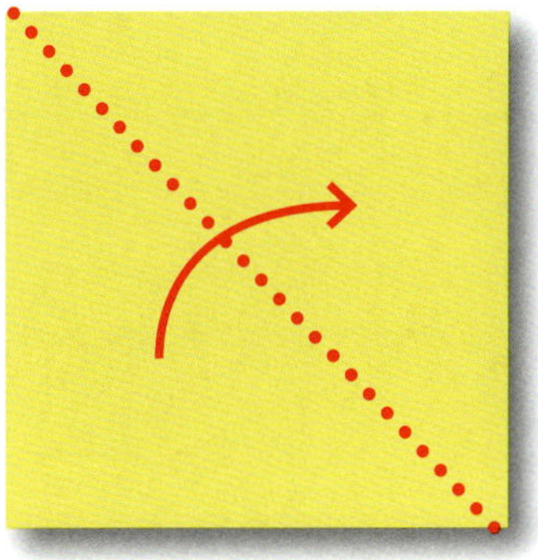

Step 2:

Now fold the two sides of the paper into the center crease to form a kite shape.

Step 3:

Fold down the top point, and crease.

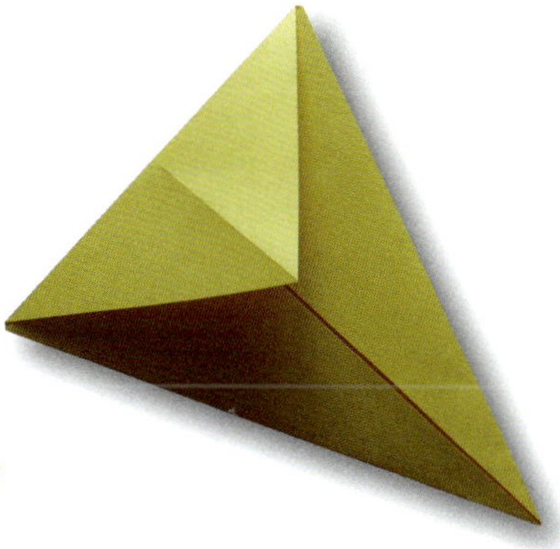

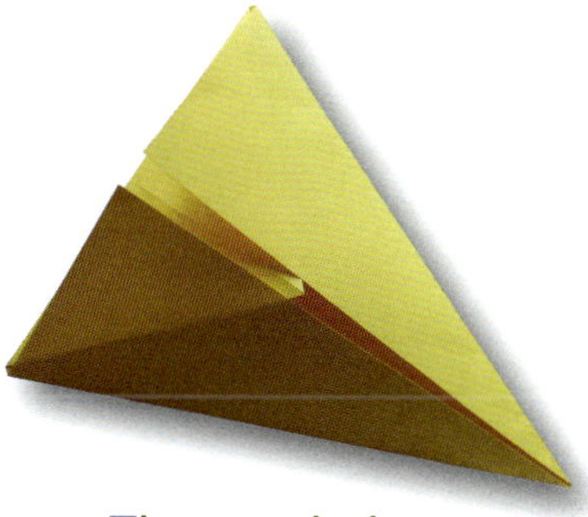

Then tuck the point inside.

Step 4:

Next, fold the top left-hand point of the model into the center, and crease.

Then fold in the top right-hand point, so that you've formed another kite shape.

Step 5:

Open out the left-hand side of the model. Then, using the folds you made in earlier steps, bring the paper together to form a pointed pocket.

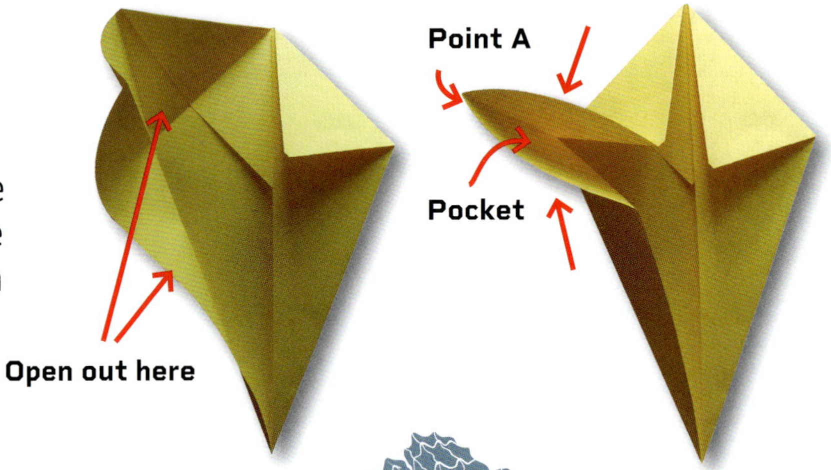

Fold down the pocket so it's flat against the model. Repeat on the right-hand side.

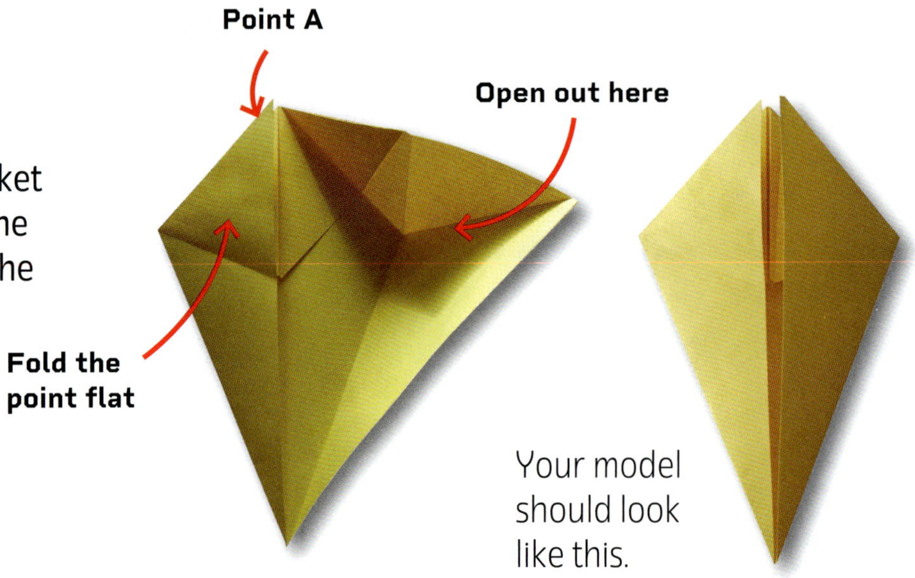

Your model should look like this.

Step 6:

Now fold up the bottom point of the model, and crease. Then fold the point back down, creating a small pleat.

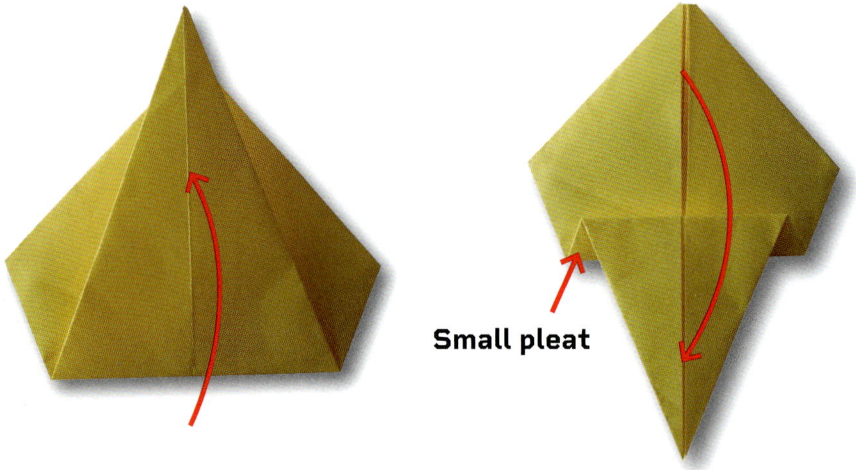

Step 7:

Fold in one side of the tail along the dotted line. As you make this fold, a small triangular pocket will form where the tail meets the body. Gently squash and flatten the triangle.

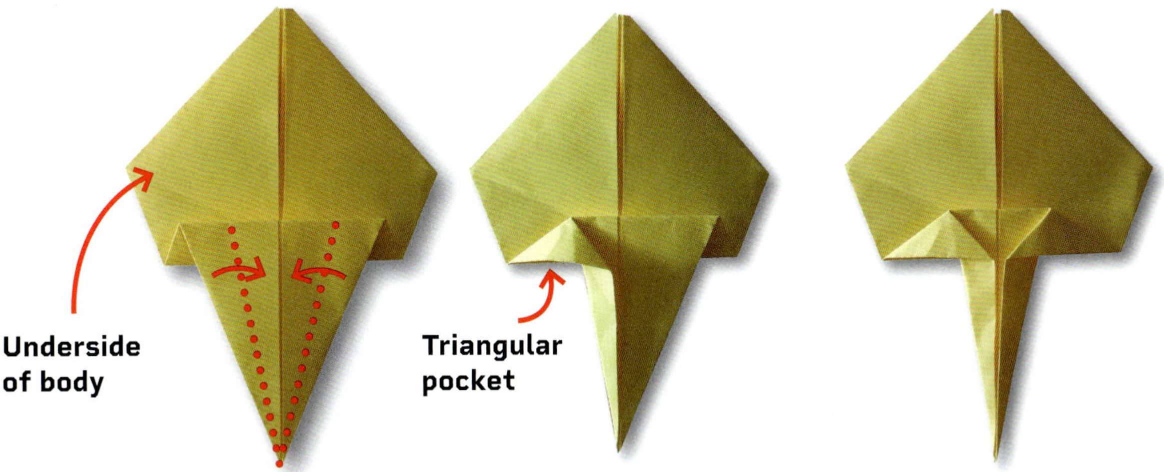

Repeat on the other side of the tail.

Step 8:

Now working with just the top layer of paper, fold down the two top points.

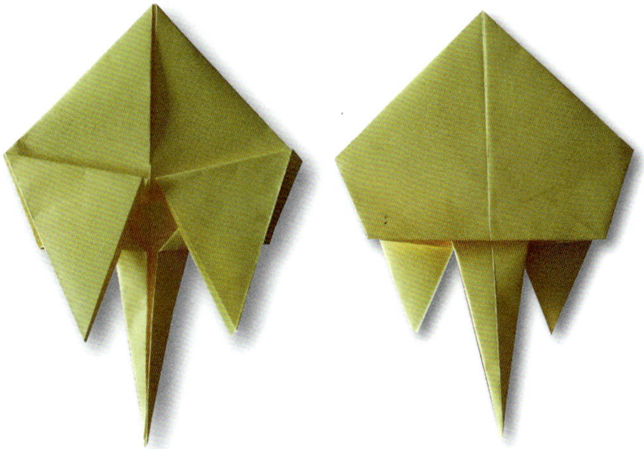

Turn the model over and it should look like this.

Step 9:

Gently squeeze the tail to make it more narrow and three-dimensional. Also, gently scrunch the center line of the body to form a ridge.

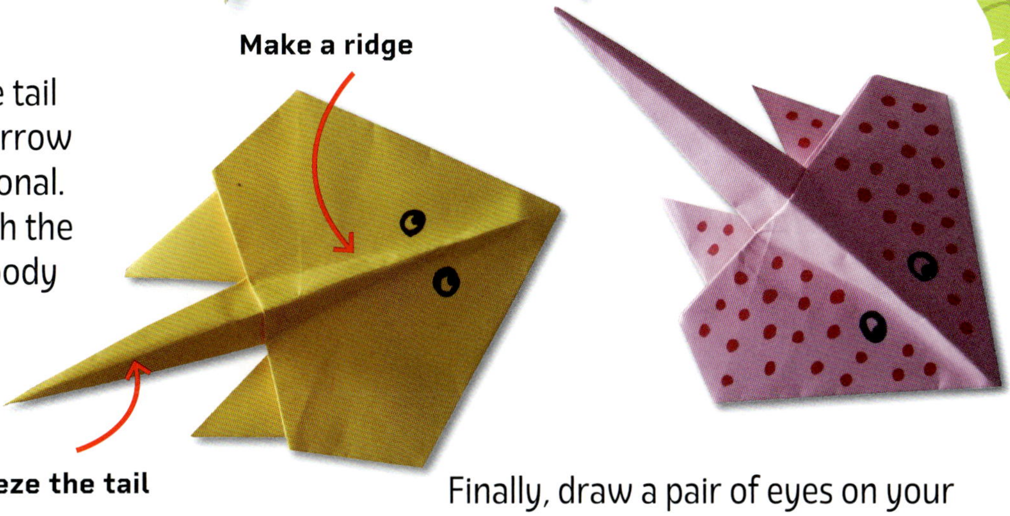

Finally, draw a pair of eyes on your stingray. You can add spots, too.

Prehistoric Hunters: Sharks

As dinosaurs stalked their prey on land, sharks hunted in the prehistoric seas. Sharks are members of the fish family that have been on Earth for around 400 million years. The dinosaurs are long gone, but sharks are still here, living and hunting in oceans around the world.

Sharks do not have bones. Instead they have a skeleton made of cartilage. This material is very strong, but it is lighter and more flexible than hard bone. Being light helps a shark float and use less energy as it moves and hunts.

A great white shark

FOLD A SHARK

You will need:

- A square piece of paper in blue or gray
- A black marker
- Scissors

Step 1:

Fold the paper in half diagonally, and crease.

Then fold the paper in half again, and crease.

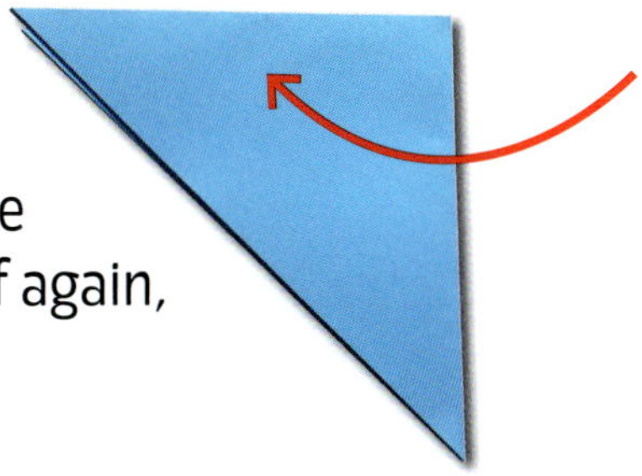

Step 2:

Now open out the top layer of paper to form a beak-like pocket.

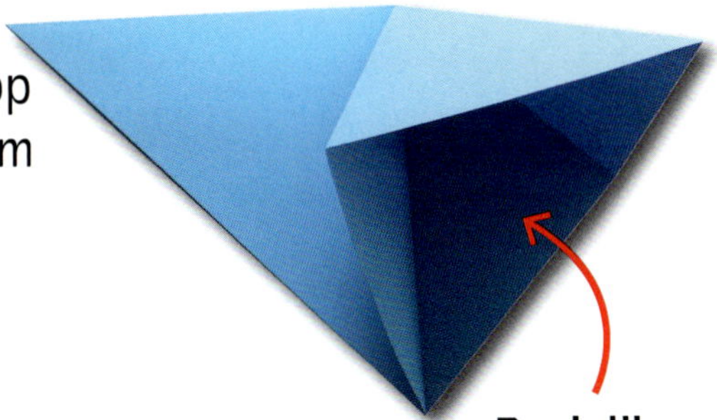

Flatten the pocket to form a square.

Step 3:

Turn the model over. Open up the right-hand point to form a beak-like pocket, and squash flat to form a square.

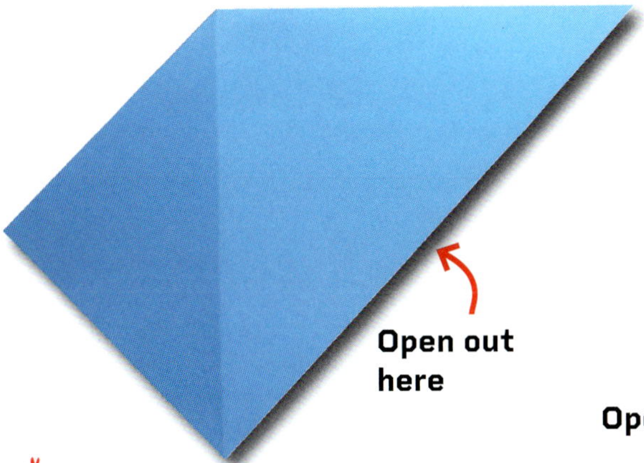

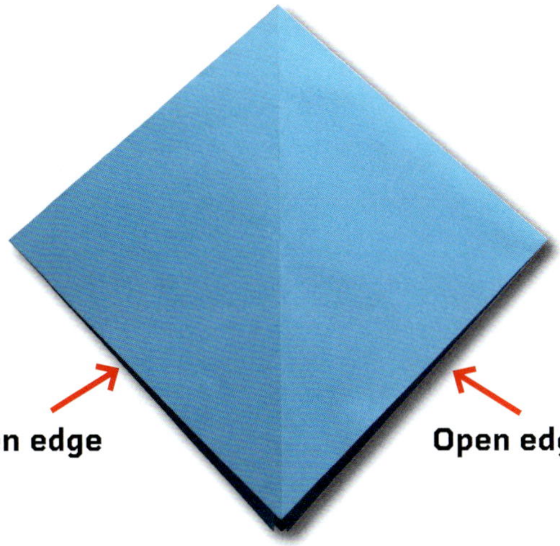

Step 4:
Working with just the top layer of paper, fold in the two side points, and crease hard.

Turn the model over, and repeat.

Fold down the top point.

Now open out the folds you've just made. The model will look a little like a bird's beak.

Squash down and flatten the model.

Step 5:
Turn the model over. Fold down the center point, crease, and then unfold.

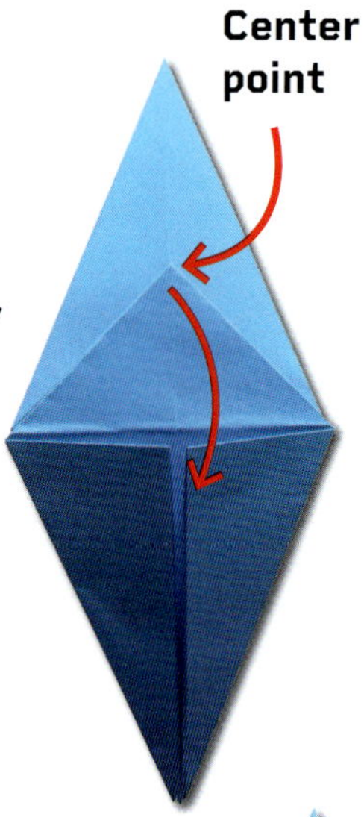

Now, repeating what you did in step 4, open out the top layer of paper to create a beak-like shape, squash down, and flatten.

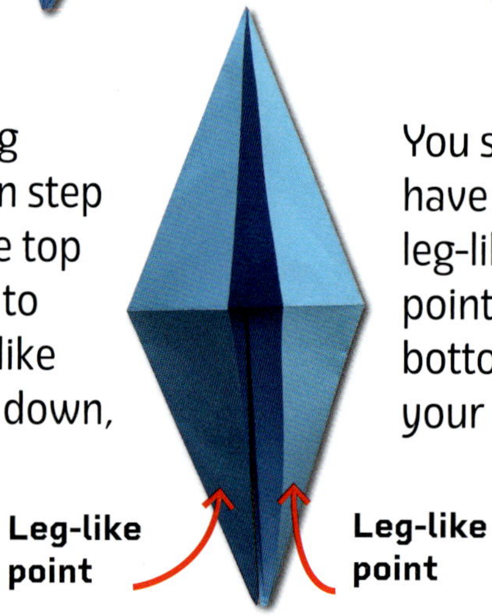

You should have two leg-like points at the bottom of your model.

Step 6:
Now, working with just the top layer of paper, fold down the top point.

Your model should look like this.

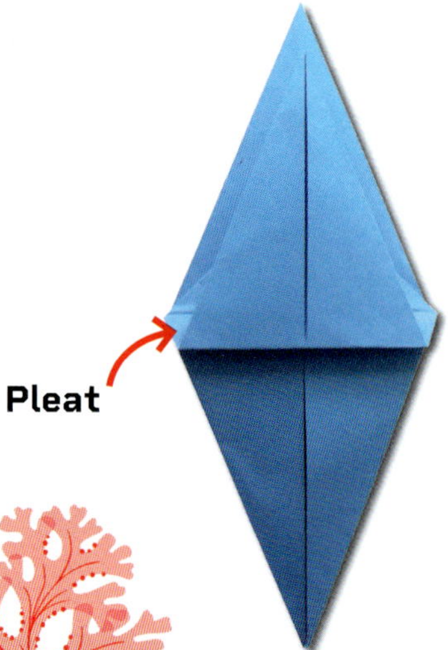

Then fold the point back up again, making a small pleat.

Step 7:

Again, working with just the top layer of paper, fold the right-hand side of the model back (like the page of a book) along the dotted line.

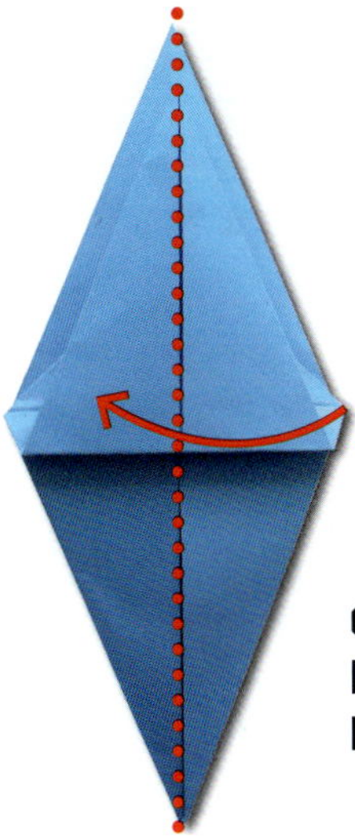

Open and fold back from here.

You should have a short point here.

Your model should now look like this.

Step 8:

Now fold up the bottom point of the model, and crease.

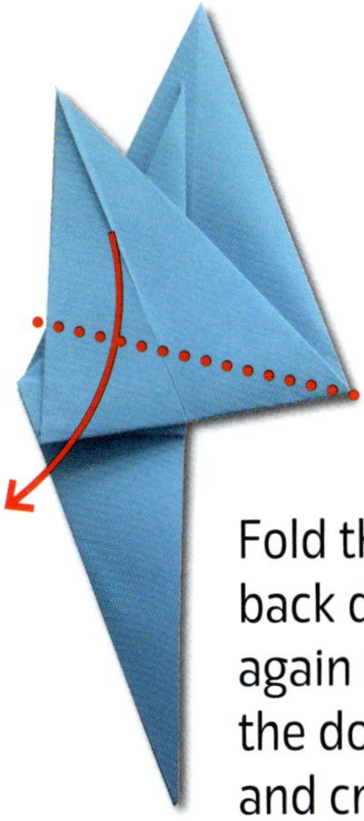

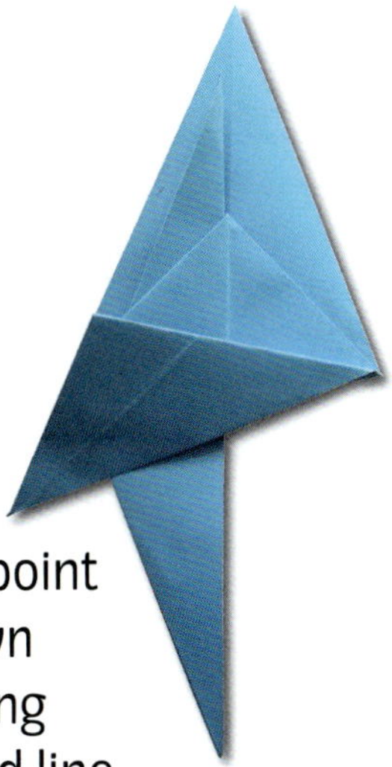

Fold the point back down again along the dotted line, and crease.

Step 9:

Now take hold of the back layer of paper on the left-hand side. Fold it behind the model toward the right-hand. If you've done this correctly, your model will look like this.

Top left-hand point

Next, take hold of the left-hand top point and gently pull it toward the left.

Step 10:

Fold, or close up, your model by folding the left-hand side to meet the right.

Turn your model 90 degrees clockwise, and it should look like this.

Step 11:

Draw on an eye and gills, and cut some jagged teeth into the shark's jaws.

Fold up the tip of the shark's tail.

Extraordinary Fish: Seahorses

Seahorses are tiny ocean creatures with horse-shaped heads that are actually fish. A male and female seahorse become partners for life. When a pair of seahorses is ready to **mate**, they put their bodies together. The female sprays hundreds of eggs into a pouch on the front of her partner's body.

Once the baby seahorses, called fry, hatch from their eggs, they live in their father's pouch for a few days. Then, once the fry are strong enough to swim, the father seahorse bends his body forward and backward. As he pushes forward, the tiny fry pop out of his pouch and swim away!

FOLD A SEAHORSE

You will need:

- A square piece of paper in your choice of color

STEP 1:

Fold the paper in half diagonally, crease, and then unfold.

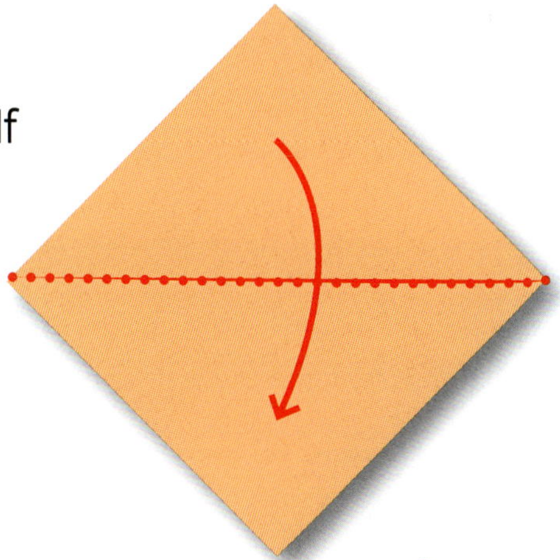

Fold the top and bottom of the paper into the center to make a kite shape, crease, and unfold.

Then fold in the top and bottom of the paper in the other direction.

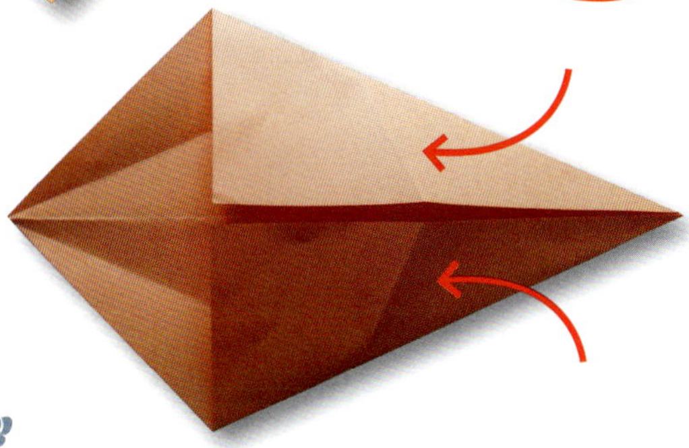

STEP 2:

Now, using the folds you made in step 1, fold in the top and bottom of the paper. As you do this, create a beak-like point at the top and bottom.

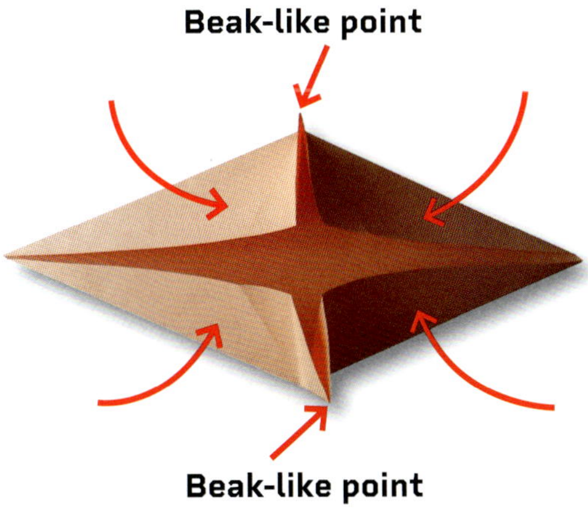

Then flatten the two beak-like points.

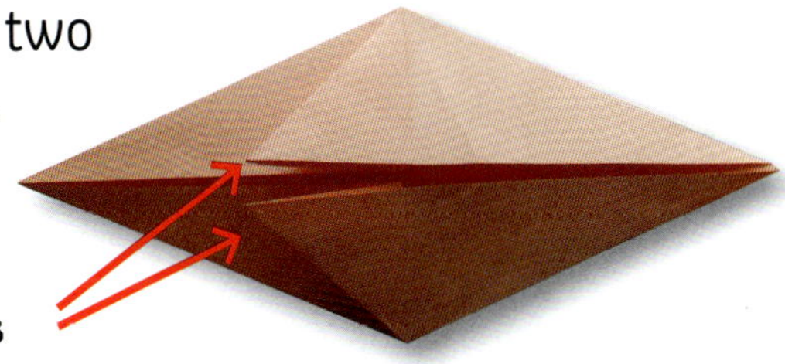

Flattened beak-like points

STEP 3:

Turn the model over and fold it in half.

Your model should look like this.

STEP 4:

Now open out the point on the side of the model and gently squash it flat. Repeat on the other side of the model.

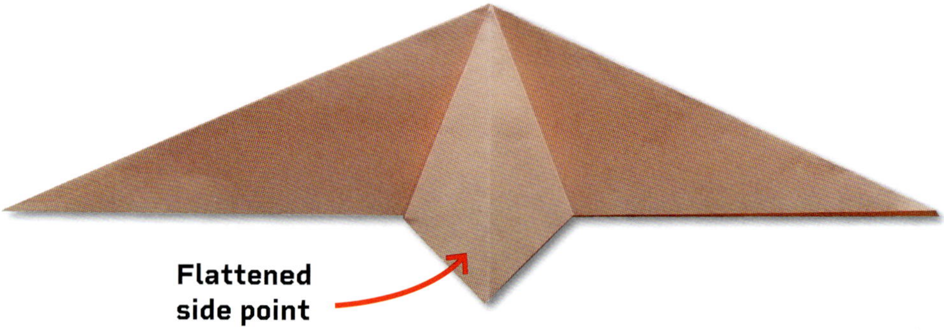

STEP 5:

Next, open up the model so you have a flat diamond shape. As you do this, make sure the two flattened side points neatly tuck beneath the model.

Now fold up the bottom of the model on the right-hand side into the center, and crease hard.

Fold down the top, and crease hard.

STEP 6:

Fold in the top and bottom of the model on the left-hand side, and crease hard.

STEP 7:

Turn the model over.

Now fold up the right-hand point of the model (toward the left), crease, and then fold back down to create a small pleat. Repeat to make a second pleat.

STEP 8:

Now pleat the left-hand point of the model twice, as you did in step 7.

Your model should now look like this.

STEP 9:

To complete your model, fold it in half along its center.

Fold over the top point to make the seahorse's head. Then fold up the tip and tuck it inside the head to create a blunt snout.

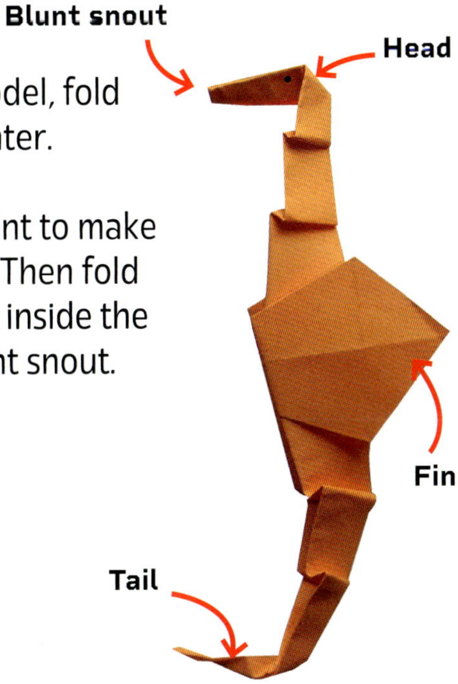

Give the seahorse's tail a gentle tug so the pleats open out slightly, allowing you to curve the tail. Curve and twist the end point of the tail.

Glossary

cartilage
Strong, rubbery tissue found in the bodies of many animals. Humans have cartilage in their noses and ears.

ectothermic
Cold-blooded and not able to maintain a constant inner body temperature.

gills
The organs of fish and some amphibians that extract oxygen from water.

larvae
The young of some animal species, including fish and insects.

mate
To come together in order to produce young.

oxygen
An invisible gas in air and in water that most living things need for survival.

predators
Animals that hunt and kill other animals for food.

prey
An animal that is hunted by another animal as food.

regulate
To adjust the temperature up or down to keep it at the same level.

species
One type of living thing. The members of a species look alike and can produce young together.

synchronized
Occurring at the same speed, time, or in the same way.

venom
A poison that is injected into a victim by a sting or bite.

vertebrates
Animals with spines, or backbones, and a skeleton of other bones.

Read More

Allan, John. *Fish (Amazing Life Cycles)*. Minneapolis, MN: Hungry Tomato, 2019.

Jacobs, Pat. *Why Do Fish Have Gills? (Wildlife Wonders)*. New York: PowerKids Press, 2017.

Markle, Sandra. *The Great Shark Rescue: Saving the Whale Sharks.* Minneapolis, MN: Millbrook Press, 2020.

Websites

https://www.nwf.org/Educational-Resources/Wildlife-Guide/fish

https://kids.nationalgeographic.com/animals/fish

https://www.deepseaworld.com/discover/animals/

Publisher's note to educators and parents: Our editors have carefully reviewed these websites to ensure that they are suitable for students. Many websites change frequently, however, and we cannot guarantee that a site's future contents will continue to meet our high standards of quality and educational value. Be advised that students should be closely supervised whenever they access the internet.

Index